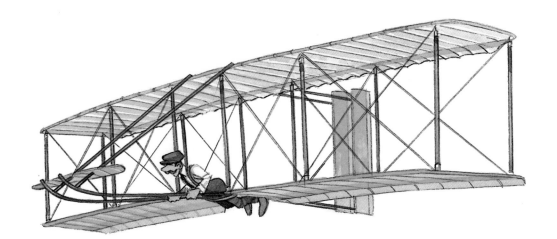

Author:
Ian Graham studied applied physics at the City University, London. He then took a postgraduate degree in journalism, specializing in science and technology. Since becoming a freelance author and journalist, he has written more than one hundred children's nonfiction books.

Artist:
David Antram was born in Brighton, England, in 1958. He studied at Eastbourne College of Art and then worked in advertising for fifteen years before becoming a full-time artist. He has illustrated many children's nonfiction books.

Series creator:
David Salariya

Editor:
Karen Barker Smith

First edition for North America (including Canada and Mexico), the Philippines, and Puerto Rico published in 2003 by Barron's Educational Series, Inc.
© The Salariya Book Company Ltd 2003

First published in Great Britain in 2003 by Book House, an imprint of
The Salariya Book Company Ltd
25 Marlborough Place, Brighton BN1 1UB

Please visit the Salariya Book Company at:
www.salariya.com
www.book-house.co.uk

All inquiries should be addressed to:
Barron's Educational Series, Inc.
250 Wireless Boulevard
Hauppauge, New York 11788
http://www.barronseduc.com

Library of Congress Catalog Card No.: 2002117624

International Standard Book No.: 0-7641-2591-5

Printed and bound in China.

Printed on paper from sustainable forests.

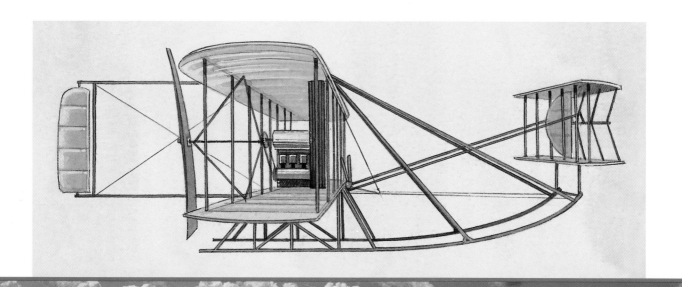

The Wright Brothers
Pioneers of flight

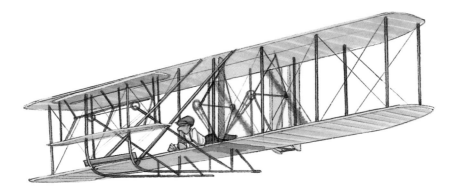

Written by
Ian Graham

Illustrated by
David Antram

The Explosion Zone

BARRON'S

Contents

Introduction

irds fly; people don't. It had been like this for as long as anyone could remember. It was the way the world was meant to be, or so most people thought. But there were a few who thought it really might be possible to build flying machines that actually flew. Some people thought they were mad. Others thought that people were never meant to fly and it was dangerous to go against the "natural order."

Orville and Wilbur Wright

By the 1890s hundreds of years of attempts to build heavier-than-air flying machines had all failed. At first, would-be aviators tried to copy nature. They hurled themselves off towers and hills wearing birdlike wings. Instead of gliding down gracefully, most of them crashed to the ground in a tangled heap. For some, it was the last thing they ever did! It seemed to be proof that humans were indeed never meant to fly. Then a handful of inventors finally began to understand the science of flight. They tried different shapes and sizes of wings and learned which was best. They built gliders that sailed on the wind. Then two unknown American brothers, Wilbur and Orville Wright, decided to try their hand at building flying machines. They would change the course of history!

Wilbur fell ill and died in 1912, aged just 45, but his brother lived until 1948, witnessing the age of the jet plane.

Inspirations

I n 1878, when Orville Wright was seven years old and his brother Wilbur was 11, their father brought home a toy helicopter. Flying toys had been made for at least 500 years. The brothers enjoyed flying their toy and even made their own copies of it. When they grew up they worked in the family's bicycle shop in Dayton, Ohio. In the 1890s newspaper stories about gliders big enough to carry a person inspired them to study flight again. They read everything they could find about flying machines and decided to try building their own. When they began, they thought they probably wouldn't be successful.

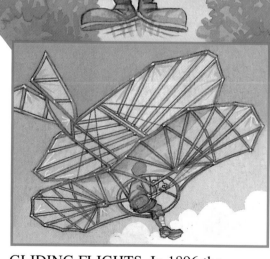

Toy helicopter like the one given to the Wright brothers

Flap flap

ORVILLE WRIGHT. Orville was born on August 19, 1871, in Dayton, Ohio.

WILBUR WRIGHT. Wilbur was born on April 16, 1867, near Millville, Indiana.

GLIDING FLIGHTS. In 1896 the brothers read about a German aviator, Otto Lilienthall, who was building his own gliders and flying them successfully.

Here's the science

Why can't we fly?

Compared to birds, we are very heavy and have no wings or a streamlined shape.

Wings and feathers

Strong chest muscles

Weak chest muscles

Heavy

Whoosh!

Creak

CONTROL. Pilots controlled their gliders by shifting their body weight. The Wright brothers thought there must be a better way to do this.

WILBUR AND ORVILLE had read about flying machines and built model aircraft since their childhood. Their father encouraged them to solve any problems they had by looking for the answers in books.

FLAPPERS. Some people tried to build full-size copies of ornithopters – flying toys with flapping wings (left). None of them worked.

On a wing and a prayer

The Wright brothers wanted to build a powered airplane, but they decided to build a glider before they tackled something with an engine. That meant designing wings. But what shape should they be? And how big? They made models to try different shapes. Then in 1899 they built a much bigger model with a wingspan of 5 feet (1.5 m). They chose a biplane design – with two wings, one wing above the other. It wasn't big enough to carry a person, but they could fly it as a kite.

Hold on to me, Wilbur!

The biplane was made from a wooden frame covered with fabric. They painted it with a type of varnish to seal the fabric so that air couldn't blow through it. When they tried it, it actually flew! In a strong gust of wind, it could lift them off the ground. Their next step was to build a glider big enough to carry a man!

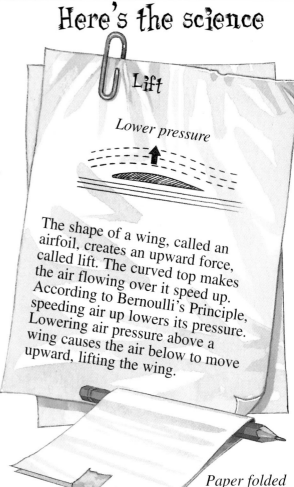

Biplane kite

Here's the science

Lift

Lower pressure

The shape of a wing, called an airfoil, creates an upward force, called lift. The curved top makes the air flowing over it speed up. According to Bernoulli's Principle, speeding air up lowers its pressure. Lowering air pressure above a wing causes the air below to move upward, lifting the wing.

Paper folded over a pencil

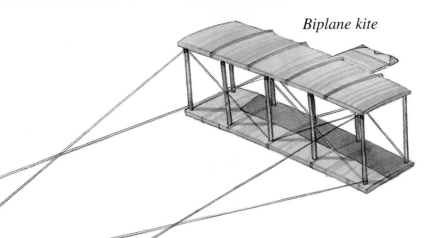

THE PERFECT PLACE. Their hometown wasn't windy enough to test gliders. They asked the U.S. Weather Bureau to help them find a windier place. They chose Kill Devil Hills, near Kitty Hawk, in North Carolina.

ATLANTIC OCEAN

PACIFIC OCEAN

Dayton

Kill Devil Hills

Try it yourself

Fold a sheet of paper over a pencil and stick the ends together. Hold the pencil level with your lower lip so that the wing hangs down. Blow down over the top of it. Blowing down makes it rise! Blowing lowers the air pressure over the wing and creates lift, pulling it upward.

Do you think it's windy enough Orville?

The first gliders

The first full-size glider built by Orville and Wilbur had a wingspan of 17 feet (5.3 m). The pilot lay on the lower wing. He climbed or dived by tilting an "elevator" at the front. The challenge was to balance the glider. If you don't balance a bicycle, it will crash, and the same is true of an aircraft. The brothers developed a balancing system of pulling wires to twist the glider's wingtips. They called it wing warping. Sadly, their glider didn't fly very well and the next one they built was even worse! Their designs relied on research done by Otto Lilienthall. They wondered if he had gotten it wrong!

Stopwatch

STOPWATCH. All of the glider flights were timed to the precise second.

A CLINOMETER was used to measure how steeply each glider climbed or dived.

Clinometer

Wheeze!

ANEMOMETER. Wind speed was measured with an anemometer. Its propeller spun and a dial showed the speed.

Tape measure

PLAGUED BY MOSQUITOES. Living at Kill Devil Hills was no picnic! Mosquitoes swarmed over the dunes ...and the brothers! Orville wrote home, "They chewed us clear through our underwear and socks. Lumps began swelling up all over my body like hen's eggs!"

TAPE MEASURE. They measured the lengths of all their flights with a tape measure.

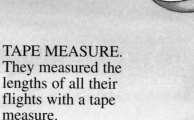

Anemometer

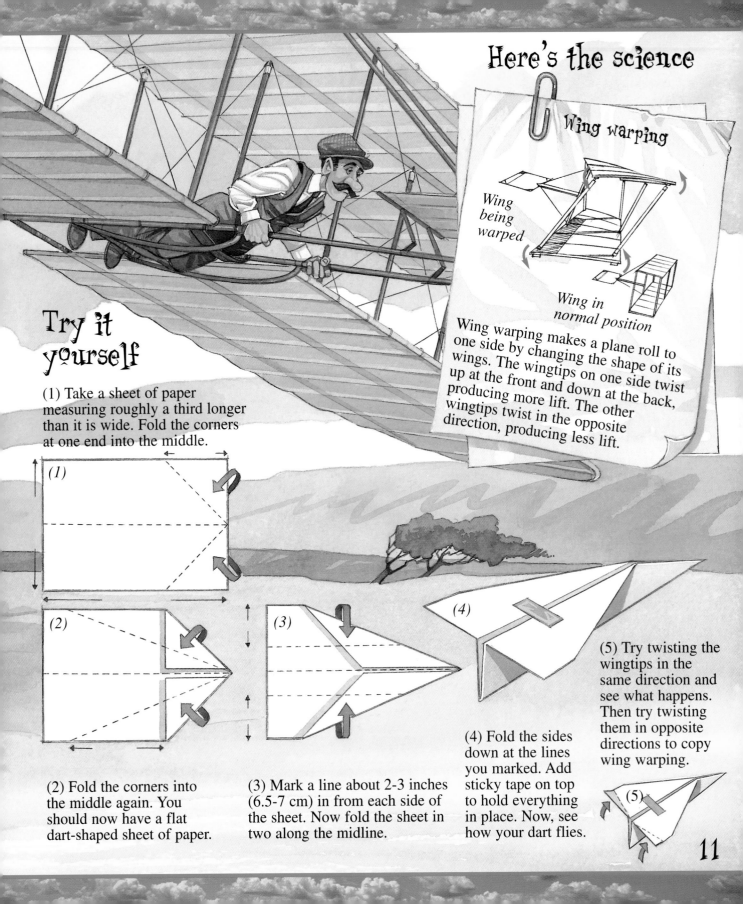

Here's the science

Wing warping

Wing being warped

Wing in normal position

Wing warping makes a plane roll to one side by changing the shape of its wings. The wingtips on one side twist up at the front and down at the back, producing more lift. The other wingtips twist in the opposite direction, producing less lift.

Try it yourself

(1) Take a sheet of paper measuring roughly a third longer than it is wide. Fold the corners at one end into the middle.

(1)

(2)

(3)

(4)

(2) Fold the corners into the middle again. You should now have a flat dart-shaped sheet of paper.

(3) Mark a line about 2-3 inches (6.5-7 cm) in from each side of the sheet. Now fold the sheet in two along the midline.

(4) Fold the sides down at the lines you marked. Add sticky tape on top to hold everything in place. Now, see how your dart flies.

(5) Try twisting the wingtips in the same direction and see what happens. Then try twisting them in opposite directions to copy wing warping.

(5)

11

Back to the drawing board

The brothers realized that they couldn't rely on facts and figures from other people so they decided to do their own research. In 1901 they went home to Dayton with notes on the flights they had made that year. They built all sorts of devices to test different shapes of wings. As they didn't have much money, everything was built using whatever materials, tools, and equipment were already on hand. This included a test machine made from a bicycle and a wind tunnel made from a wooden box, a fan, and their workshop motor. Armed with their own research results, they started work on designing a completely new glider.

BICYCLE TEST RIG. The bicycle had an extra wheel on top with a flat plate on one side and a model wing, standing on end, on the other side. As the bicycle was ridden, wind hitting the plate and the wing tried to turn the wheel in opposite directions. By trying different model wings and seeing how much the wheel turned, the Wright brothers could tell which wing was best.

Model wing

Flat plate

12 *Bicycle test rig*

Wind tunnel

WIND TUNNEL. The most useful of the Wright's test machines was a wind tunnel. A fan blew air through it at approximately 30 mph (48 kph), so that they could test different-shaped wings.

Here's the science

Stalling

→ Direction of flight

If a plane's nose tips up too far, air cannot flow smoothly over its wings. Lift suddenly disappears and the plane dives. This is called stalling.

Wright brothers' workshop

Perfection!

No. 3 glider

n 1902 Orville and Wilbur went back to Kitty Hawk with a new glider, their *No. 3*. This had been designed using the results of their latest research and tests. Its wings were longer and thinner than earlier gliders and it had two tall vanes at the back. It flew better than their previous designs, but there were still a few problems to iron out. They found it flew better with the wingtips a little closer together and the tail needed some changes to make it easier to control in turns. By the time they'd finished with it, *No. 3* was the world's first fully controllable aircraft. It was so successful that they decided they were ready to move on to the next step – building a powered aircraft.

THE No. 3 WRIGHT GLIDER of 1902 looked slender and graceful because of its longer, thinner wings (above). After all the research that went into its design, it flew beautifully too.

However, *No. 3* could be tricky in turns. In one, it slid sideways and slammed into the ground. Luckily the pilot, Orville, was dazed but uninjured.

daze   spin

I think we need to look at the tail.

Pitch, roll, and yaw

An aircraft can move in three different ways – pitch, roll, and yaw.

YAW. An aircraft yaws when its nose turns to the left or right.

PITCH. An aircraft's pitch changes when its nose rises or falls.

ROLL. An aircraft rolls, or banks, when one wing rises and the other falls.

TURNING PROBLEM. The brothers discussed how to solve the problem of sliding in turns by changing the glider's tail.

RUDDER. They decided to change the tail so that it had one moveable vane, a rudder (right), instead of two fixed vanes, to give the pilot more control in turns.

THE TAIL was finally linked to the wing-warping cradle (below). Now, when the glider rolled, the tail swiveled automatically and kept the aircraft under control. Perfection!

Wing-warping cradle

Elevator control

Bonk!

Rudder swivels when wings warp

Power

t was calculated that the brothers needed an 8-horsepower engine weighing up to 181 pounds (82 kg) to power their new aircraft. They thought they would be able to buy one from one of the many engine-making companies they knew. But when the time came, they couldn't get what they wanted. So, they decided to build the engine themselves! Their bicycle mechanic, Charles Taylor, helped with the design and then built it for them. It had four cylinders and burned ordinary gasoline. It was ready for testing in only six weeks. Their engine was good enough for the short test-flights they were planning – if their aircraft took off!

WANTED – ONE ENGINE. They wrote to suppliers with details of the engine they needed. But none was able to supply the right engine at the right price.

BUILD IT YOURSELF. Their mechanic, Charles Taylor, built their engine without any detailed plans (above). They sketched the parts they needed and Taylor made them. Amazingly, it actually worked!

Here's the science

Gasoline engine

Cylinder

Piston

Shaft

When a gasoline engine starts, gas is sprayed into each of its cylinders. A spark makes the fine mist of gasoline burn. The gases produced heat up and expand. They push a piston down the cylinder. The up-down movements of the pistons turn a shaft.

SUCCESS! The finished engine was lighter and more powerful than they expected. Because of this, they were able to make the plane heavier and stronger and it would still take off – they hoped!

Engine made by Charles Taylor and the Wright brothers

Spinning props

An engine cannot fly an airplane by itself. A propeller is needed to push an aircraft through the air. Orville and Wilbur thought they could simply redesign ship propellers to produce a propeller that worked in air. But they were amazed to find that ship propellers were made by trial and error! They first had to work out how ship propellers functioned before designing their own propellers. They decided to use two, driven by chains from the engine. Mounting the propellers behind the wings meant that they wouldn't spoil the smooth air flow over the wings.

So why are they this shape, Orville?

What do you mean, I have a terrible temper!

You have a terrible temper!

ARGUMENTS. The two brothers were great arguers. They often thrashed out tricky problems by shouting at each other at the top of their voices!

SHIP PROPELLERS.
The two brothers wanted to base their airplane propellers on ship propellers. The trouble was no one had worked out how to design them. Even the people who made ship propellers didn't know why they were the shape they were!

THE WRIGHT PROPELLERS WERE TESTED (below) to make sure their theories and calculations were correct. Each wooden propeller was 9 feet (2.6 m) from tip to tip.

Here's the science

How a propeller works

A propeller is like a set of whirling wings. As its blades cut through air, the air pressure drops in front and rises behind, forcing the plane through the sky.

Propeller

They don't seem to know, Wilbur!

Whirr

Building the Flyer

The Wright brothers' first powered aircraft, the *Flyer*, had a wooden frame and a wingspan of 40 feet (12.3 m). There were two elevators at the front and two rudders at the back. The wings, elevators, and rudders were covered with fabric. The engine was mounted on the lower wing. But there was still no seat! The pilot lay in a cradle that slid from side to side to warp the wings. There were no wheels either! The *Flyer* rested on a trolley on a long rail. When the plane took off, the trolley fell away. When it landed again, it simply skidded to a halt on the ground.

Flyer

MAKING A WING. *Flyer*'s wings were made from wooden ribs running from front to back. These were fixed to beams called spars running the length of the wings, with cloth stretched over the top and bottom surfaces.

Wooden rib

Wooden spar

Fabric covering

The beauty of wood

The brothers made their aircraft from wood because it was cheap and available, but also because it was strong and flexible. It could bend without breaking.

THE TAKEOFF RAIL had to be laid on level ground. Luckily, the sandy, uneven ground (right) was leveled by recent flooding – perfect for the track.

The first flight...ever!

Preparations for the first flight were made on the morning of December 14, 1903. The brothers tossed a coin for who would pilot the *Flyer*. Wilbur won. He lay down in the warp cradle and the engine was started. The plane moved away down the launch rail, gathered speed and lifted off. Then disaster! It plowed into the sand! It was December 17 before they could try again. It was Orville's turn to be pilot. Five other people witnessed this attempt. This time, the plane sailed away into the wind and landed 12 seconds later, aproximately 120 feet (36 m) away. They made three more flights that day. They had made history!

THE FIRST ATTEMPT to make a flight failed and the plane was damaged. Wilbur, who was piloting the plane, was unhurt.

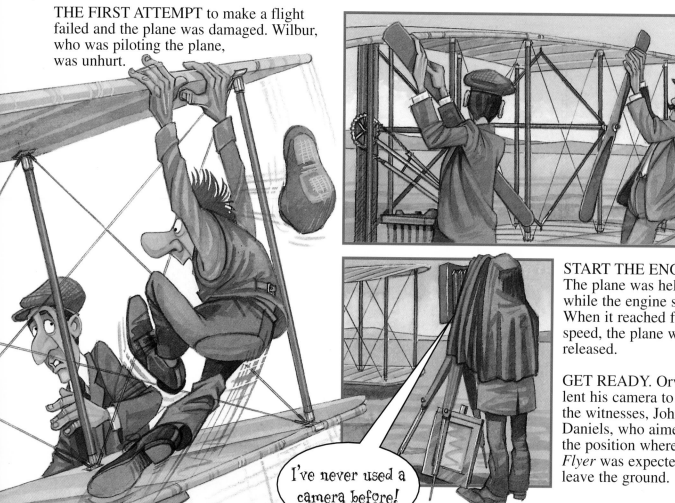

I've never used a camera before!

START THE ENGINE. The plane was held while the engine started. When it reached full speed, the plane was released.

GET READY. Orville lent his camera to one of the witnesses, John Daniels, who aimed it at the position where the *Flyer* was expected to leave the ground.

Image of the first flight, December 17, 1903

Daniels pressed the button at the right moment to take a historic photograph (similar to the image above) of the first-ever airplane flight!

Here's the science

Airplane forces

Lift

Drag

Thrust

Weight

The same four forces act on all airplanes, including the Wright *Flyer* – weight, lift, thrust, and drag.

Lift from the wings pulls the plane upward; thrust from the propellers pushes the plane forward; drag, or air resistance, tries to slow the plane down; weight due to gravity pulls the plane down.

They done it! They done it!

And now, next year's model

Making history would be enough for most people, but not Wilbur and Orville Wright! Now they built a series of new planes, each improving on the one before. The first was *Flyer II*, built in 1904. Engine power meant that they didn't need strong winds to take off, so they left Kitty Hawk and started flying at Huffman Prairie, closer to their home in Dayton. In 1905 they built *Flyer III*. This was the first really practical airplane and they finally had an aircraft that could make longer flights. They could bank, turn, fly in circles, make figures of eight, whatever they wanted. *Flyer III*'s longest flight lasted for 38 minutes.

FLYER II. The Wright brothers used *Flyer II* to learn how to control a plane in the air. Then they thought they could improve on it. So they built yet another plane and called it *Flyer III*!

THE END OF THE ORIGINAL FLYER. Later in the same day as its first historic flights, the original *Flyer* was hit by a gust of wind. John Daniels tried to hold it down, but it turned over, injuring him. *Flyer* was damaged so badly that it never flew again.

Spot the difference

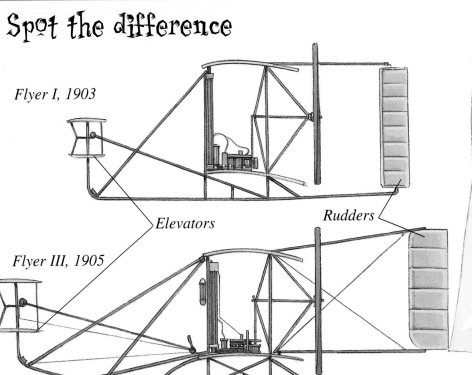

Flyer I, 1903

Elevators

Rudders

Flyer III, 1905

Compared to the original *Flyer*, *Flyer III* had its elevators further forward and its rudders further back. Making the plane longer made it easier for the pilot to control it.

Pulleys

Pulleys are useful for changing the direction of a force. The Wright brothers used them to change the down, or vertical, force of a weight into a side, or horizontal, force to pull an aircraft along its launch rail.

Vertical force

Horizontal force

RAISING THE LAUNCH-SYSTEM WEIGHT. Before each flight, the 1,760-pound (800 kg) weight had to be raised to the top of the tower (right). It was usually done by a group of volunteers pulling on a rope. Then the rope was hooked up to the plane.

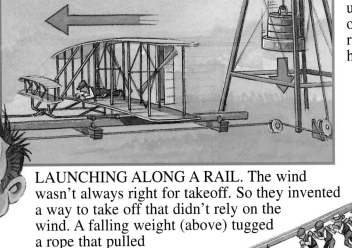

LAUNCHING ALONG A RAIL. The wind wasn't always right for takeoff. So they invented a way to take off that didn't rely on the wind. A falling weight (above) tugged a rope that pulled the airplane along its launch-rail.

Launch system with weight, pulleys, and rail

Look! He's flying!

Take a seat

In 1907 the Wright brothers finally built an airplane with a seat! The *Type A*, as it became known, was an improved version of *Flyer III*. Not only did it have a seat for the pilot, but also a passenger seat. The first airplane passengers experienced the magic of flight in 1908. They sat on the wing with the pilot, so it was a very windy experience. That could cause problems, because of the fashion of the day. Any woman who flew as a passenger had to have her long skirt tied around with string to preserve her modesty! Now that the pilot was sitting up and not lying in a warp cradle, he couldn't slide to each side to warp the wings and bank (roll) the plane. Instead, he used control sticks to move the rudders, wings, and elevators.

Flight controls

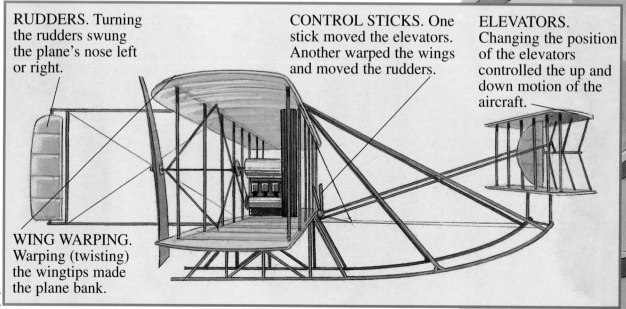

RUDDERS. Turning the rudders swung the plane's nose left or right.

CONTROL STICKS. One stick moved the elevators. Another warped the wings and moved the rudders.

ELEVATORS. Changing the position of the elevators controlled the up and down motion of the aircraft.

WING WARPING. Warping (twisting) the wingtips made the plane bank.

Here's the science

Banking

An airplane has to bank, or roll to one side, to make a turn, just like leaning a bicycle to make a turn. When a plane banks, some of the lift from its wings pulls it sideways into the turn.

Modern airplanes

Compared to the Wright *Flyer*, a modern airliner has its elevators and rudder in its tail, and uses ailerons (see page 29) to steer instead of wing warping.

Showing the world

The Wright brothers showed the world their invention in 1908. Wilbur made flights in France, while Orville showed the plane to the U.S. Army. The army had been offered a Wright plane in 1905, but they thought the idea of military airplanes was ridiculous! All went well until Orville took Lieutenant T.E. Selfridge up for a flight. Disaster struck – they crashed and Selfridge was killed. The army bought the plane anyway. Meanwhile, in France, people didn't believe reports of the Wright brothers' success. When they saw Wilbur flying so gracefully, they were amazed. Count de La Vaulx said the Wright plane "revolutionized the aviator's world."

WILBUR'S FLIGHTS IN FRANCE were front-page news everywhere. This magazine cover (above) shows him flying at Hunaudières Racecourse, near Le Mans, in 1908.

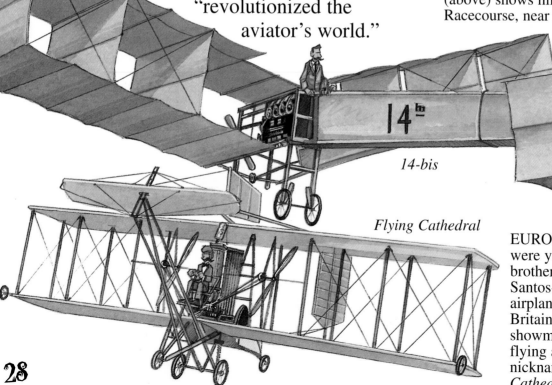

14-bis

Flying Cathedral

EUROPEAN AVIATORS were years behind the Wright brothers. In France, Alberto Santos-Dumont built an odd airplane called *14-bis*. In Britain, the Wild West showman, Colonel Cody, was flying a huge airplane nicknamed the *Flying Cathedral*!

The world's first crash investigation

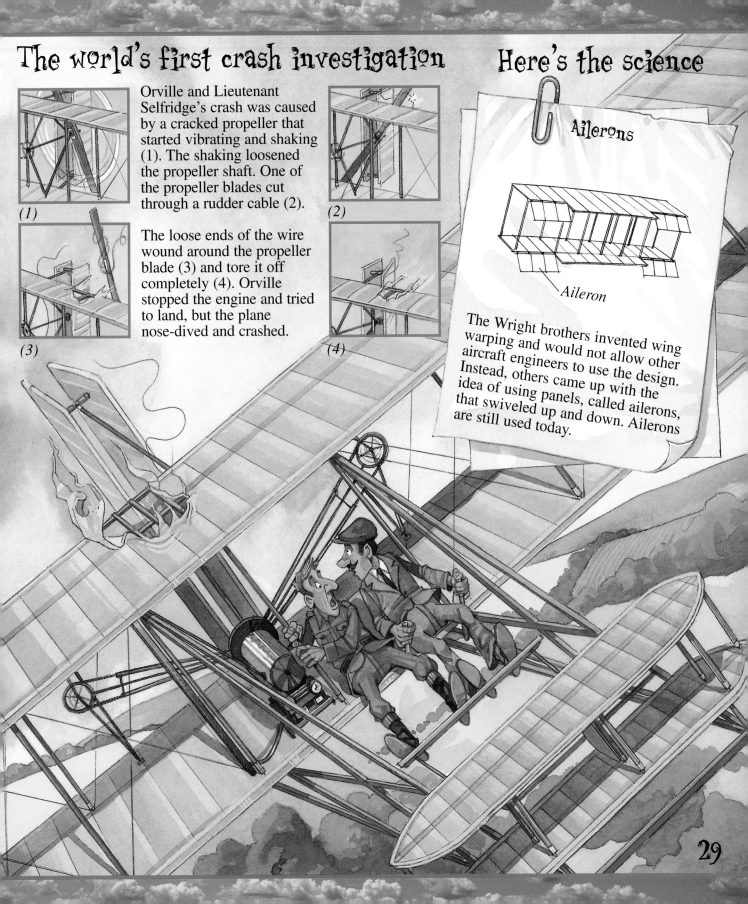

Orville and Lieutenant Selfridge's crash was caused by a cracked propeller that started vibrating and shaking (1). The shaking loosened the propeller shaft. One of the propeller blades cut through a rudder cable (2).

The loose ends of the wire wound around the propeller blade (3) and tore it off completely (4). Orville stopped the engine and tried to land, but the plane nose-dived and crashed.

(1)

(2)

(3)

(4)

Here's the science

Ailerons

Aileron

The Wright brothers invented wing warping and would not allow other aircraft engineers to use the design. Instead, others came up with the idea of using panels, called ailerons, that swiveled up and down. Ailerons are still used today.

Glossary

Ailerons Parts of an aircraft's wings that swivel up or down to make the plane roll or bank.

Airfoil The special shape of a wing, designed to produce lift.

Anemometer An instrument for measuring wind speed.

Aviator An old-fashioned word for a flier or pilot.

Banking Rolling an aircraft over to one side to make a turn.

Clinometer An instrument for measuring how steep a slope is.

Cylinder The tube-shaped part inside a gasoline engine where the gas is burned.

Drag A force that tries to slow down an aircraft, caused by air pressing against the aircraft as it flies along.

Elevator The part of an aircraft that tilts to make the plane climb or dive.

Glider An aircraft designed to fly without an engine.

Lift The upward force produced by a wing that makes an airplane rise into the air.

Piston Part of a gasoline engine that moves up and down inside a cylinder and turns the engine's main shaft.

Pitch A movement of an aircraft that makes its nose rise or fall.

Rib Part of the frame inside a wing that runs from the front of the wing to the back.

Roll A movement of an aircraft that makes one wing rise and the other fall.

Rudder The part of an airplane's tail that swivels from side to side to make the plane's nose turn to the left or right.

Shaft A spinning rod in an engine.

Spar Part of the frame of an airplane's wing that runs the length of the wing.

Stall A sudden loss of lift caused by flying too slowly or raising an aircraft's nose too high.

Thrust The force that pushes an airplane through the air.

Vane An aircraft part in the shape of a fin or flat panel.

Warp cradle The wooden frame that the pilot of a Wright glider lay in and slid to one side or the other to make the aircraft bank.

Wind tunnel A tube or chamber through which air is blown by a fan, to test wings and other aircraft parts.

Wing Part of an aircraft designed to produce lift when it cuts through air.

Wing warping Twisting a plane's wingtips to make it roll or bank.

Yaw A movement of an aircraft that makes its nose turn to the right or left.

Index